FOOD FOR THOUGHT

THE ANIMATED STORY OF AN INSPIRING CUPCAKE

series one

SANDE MILLER REAL

REAL EXPRESSIONS PUBLISHING CO.
Snohomish, WA

Library of Congress Catalog Card Number 95-092437

ISBN 0- 9647708-0-6

ACKNOWLEDGEMENTS

I gratefully acknowledge the contributions of Ken Proctor in supporting this book to its completion, and for the "Pearls of Wisdom". His caring has been vital, as has that of my daughters, Lea Sheppard and Rae Ramage. I also want to thank my granddaughter, Rachel, for stimulating my story telling once again.

Special thanks go to my friends, Manuela Adelman of Parma, Italy, and Shakti Gawain and her husband, Jim Burns, for acknowledging the power of my own unique form of expression; to Sammie Proud, a fellow artist, whose enthusiasm gave me support for continuing my work; to Annie Crespo, my friend and massage therapist, who helped me see the blue light; and to Jana Lyons, for her expert work making all my drawings and dialogue camera ready. And finally, to Pete Satterlee, who remembered a part of me that had been long forgotten, my artist.

INTRODUCTION

Hi! My name is C.C. I live with my friends among you. But the only place you can see me is on these pages. I'm your imagination, your wisdom, your feelings and experiences.

I'm food for thought.

FOREWORD

From what walks of life
do we cherish ourselves
the most.

Is it the simplicity of
conforming to standards
set by others who have
gone before us, and live
around us;
or is it taking steps outside
our machine paved concrete,
which sets us over a course
of bumps and falls
as we envision a new
trail to our
innermost/outermost
sense of who we are,
and how much we can
be.

Sometimes to break out of
the mold of normalcy,
to which we at times
try to adhere-
we have to do something
extraordinary . . .

Like enter a parallel
universe.

IV FOOD FOR THOUGHT

Such a place exists around us, which vibrates so fast that what we consider inanimate can come to life. It is a world like our own, inhabited by C.C. Cupcake and others, where they reflect ourselves, as if we're looking into a mirror.

They do have one special quality we do not. When they choose to slow their vibrational rate, they can exist with humans; animals can do this, too, shifting between C.C.'s world and our own. It is a rare gift; how fortunate they are to be able to experience another reality and then return to their own.

Of course, we have attempted to do the same - by telling stories. Myths, fairy tales, folklore, plays, even humor, have excited our imaginations for generations, informing us about ourselves and allowing us to "see" and feel, like images in dreams, with less reliance on perfect explanations.

Do you remember a time when you explored thoughts and ideas without being deadly serious about reaching a logical conclusion, or being politically correct? Or having to remember every detailed explanation and bit of information in order to believe you "got it"? Today it appears we have become data junkies, where details fly at us fast and furious and every point of view seems to have an answer for what we need to, or should do. And we are struggling with the limits this creates. It is not right - nor wrong - just what we have learned to do.

So perhaps it is time to surprise yourself again - like those times when your imagination crept up on you and gave you moments of enjoyment and insight - and allow C.C.'s world to take you on a trail of exploring in a different form.

Her story begins with a phone call in the middle of the night, and this call starts to reveal a familiar role she has in her family - caretaker, confidante, and problem solver. The power of her role will extend to her work, and soon to her relationship with Peter Pickle.

In "doing good for others", C.C. encounters life as we do - family problems, work difficulties, social issues; and she decides to try and figure it all out, as many of us do, with various ideas, therapies, and methods. She is hopeful, gets hurt, feels, tries hard, and is dedicated to making things better. But along the way, she also misses cues of what it means to be complete, to sense and know one's self.

She is a product of her popular culture - that by going beyond the call of duty and denying what she needs to feel, and deal with, she will get a happier, easier path in life. Her conflicts, however, will not go away, and she has to discover her need to individuate before coming full circle back into how she wishes to be in relationships.

In a rhythm with C.C.'s experiences are Pearls of Wisdom, places in the story to pause and ponder about what is occurring. They are a bridge between herself and our own realization that there are more ways to consider being in life than we may have imagined. They are timely and challenging, and confirm that we can change out of our conflicts.

Which, after all, is what C.C. encounters as she finds self-actualization, reveals more of herself, deals with the subtleties, behaviors and agendas of others, and expresses the weaknesses, imperfections, strengths and comedy being "human" implies.

MENU

ONCE UPON A TIME,

ON A DARK AND DREARY NIGHT,

AT EXACTLY 12:01 AM,

SUDDENLY, A PHONE RINGS.

Boom!
ZZZ
RING RING!
Ant Acid

CC?
THIS IS SIS. TATER TOT HASN'T COME HOME. I JUST KNOW HE'S DRUGGING AND DRINKING. WHAT SHOULD I DO?
SNORE!

TATER IS TURNING OUT JUST LIKE HIS FATHER. YA KNOW, MOTHER WAS RIGHT. I NEVER SHOULD HAVE MARRIED OUTSIDE MY OWN FOOD GROUP.
MOM
SNORT!

WE'VE ALREADY TRIED EVERYTHING. HE WOULDN'T STAY IN TREATMENT, WON'T GO TO MEETINGS. . . . MAYBE I CAN HELP BY ATTENDING SOME MEETINGS MYSELF.
THANKS, BIG SISTER. I JUST KNEW YOU WOULDN'T LET ME DOWN. I'D GO CRAZY IF I DIDN'T HAVE YOU TO LEAN ON. MOM WAS RIGHT WHEN SHE SAID, "DON'T TAKE YOUR PROBLEMS OUTSIDE THE FAMILY". DID I TELL YOU I'M LOOKING FOR A JOB, ALTHOUGH OL' POTATO HEAD HERE DOESN'T WANT ME TO WORK. . . BLAH, BLAH, BLAH.

CC? ARE
YOU THERE?
HELLO?
HELLO!

NEXT DAY, C.C. AT WORK
HI! A PENNY FOR YOUR THOUGHTS?
OH MY, THE CLAIMS CLERK WAS RIGHT, MR. CUKE. YOUR MANAGED CARE COMPANY DOESN'T ALLOW THE OPERATION YOU NEED TO SAVE YOUR LIFE.
ONE CENT
10 CENTS
ROLL
BURRITO
I ♥ NY
MS. CUPCAKE, ADM. ASST.

WAAAAH!
EEEK!
ONE CENT
ENTS
NY
MS. CUPCAKE, ADM. ASST.

BOO HOO HOO
THERE, THERE, DON'T WORRY, I'LL FIGURE SOMETHING OUT.
PAT PAT
MS.
PCAKE, ADM. ASST.
I ♥ NY

C.C. CAN'T EXPECT TO STAY IN MANAGEMENT VERY LONG WITH SUCH A DESPICABLE ATTITUDE AS COMPASSION.
PLEASE STOP CRYING. I'LL FIX IT, I PROMISE.
sniff sniff!
MS. CUPCAKE, ADM.
WELL, SO MUCH FOR THE INDIVIDUAL NEEDS OF THE PATIENT. IF I DIDN'T NEED THIS JOB, I'D QUIT.

Are we too eager to repel
a touch which might quiver,
a sight of tears flowing,
a desire to be held,
a thought needing to disagree?

Or do we have to fix everything.

LIFE'S NOT FAIR...AND THESE HEELS ARE KILLING ME.
ROUGH DAY, HUH? SEE YOU TOMORROW, C.C.
one cent
GARAGE LEVEL NO. 3

EARLY NEXT MORNING

RING! RING!
RING! RING!

NO, SIS,
I HAVEN'T GOTTEN
TO A MEETING YET.

IT'S BEEN LESS
THAN 24 HOURS SINCE
I TALKED TO YOU....
YES, OKAY, I'LL DO IT
TOMORROW. MY DAY
OFF, I MIGHT ADD.....
ME, UPSET? NO, OF
COURSE NOT.

Pretending to not feel
what you already feel
takes a lot of time
and effort -

Sometimes it's called
passive/aggressive behavior.

That's like a big dog
standing with his paws
on someone's shoulders,
licking her face and
peeing on her leg
at the same time.

SATURDAY MORNING

DRIVING UNDER THE INFLUENCE
MEETING

THEY SEEM HARMLESS ENOUGH,
ALTHOUGH THEY DON'T LOOK
ANYTHING LIKE ME . . . OR TATER,
FOR THAT MATTER.

JUST BECAUSE I HAVE NINE DUI'S DOESN'T MEAN I HAVE A PROBLEM WITH ALCOHOL OR DRUGS!
WHAT I HEAR YOU SAYING IS, YOU THINK WE'RE A BUNCH OF IDIOTS.

LEAVE IT TO AN OVERRIPE PIECE OF FRUIT TO SCREW UP THE WHOLE GROUP.
DON'T THINK I'LL BE SAYING ANYTHING ANYTIME SOON . . .
SOME THERAPIST. WHAT A SANCTIMONIOUS, A-NUMBER ONE JERK!
IT'S TIMES LIKE THIS I WISH I HAD A DRINK.

ARE YOU REFERRING TO ME, SIR? I DON'T HAVE ANY PROBLEMS!
whip!
SO, PETER PICKLE, TELL ME ABOUT THE EXCESS ENERGY IN YOUR LEG. WHAT'S THAT REALLY ABOUT?
TAP!
TAP!!!
TAP!
TAP

OH,...
I SEE YOU DECIDED
THIS WOULD BE AN
INTERESTING
EXPERIENCE,
ATTENDING A DUI GROUP FILLED
WITH HOSTILITY AND DENIAL.
AND HERE I THOUGHT YOU
CAME TO TRY TO GET YOUR
DRIVER'S LICENSE BACK BY
YOUR ATTENDANCE, AND
HOPEFULLY LEARN SOME
SELF-AWARENESS IN THE
PROCESS. HMM, VERY
INTERESTING.

WELL, ACTUALLY I CAME HERE BECAUSE I THOUGHT IT WOULD BE AN INTERESTING EXPERIENCE. I MEAN, WELL, I DON'T DRINK OR TAKE DRUGS...OR... ANYTHING.
GET A GRIP, HONEY!
AH,...BATHROOM..PLEASE?

READ MY LIPS!
YOU'RE IN DENIAL!
...HEH...HEH...HEH

AND WHILE I'M AT IT, THAT LITTLE GUY ACROSS FROM ME KEEPS TAKING BATHROOM BREAKS, WITH HIS BRIEFCASE?!?! COME ON, GROUP, GET A GRIP! HE'S DRINKING - YOU KNOW IT, I KNOW IT ... SO WHAT ARE WE GOING TO DO ABOUT HIM!
WE? SO YOU'RE SPEAKING FOR THE WHOLE GROUP? HMMM ... INTERESTING.

BELCH!
NOW WOULD BE A GOOD TIME TO CLOSE. NEXT WEEK'S TOPIC - REPRESSED EMOTIONS AND THE DRUG DEPENDENT PERSONALITY.

If you think the light
has failed you, remember
the stars you see when
something hits you
between the eyes.

It is not misfortune
to be confronted;
it is more likely
you'll gain a map
to buried treasure.

A word of caution:
If you continue to believe
that gold is worthless,
you may wind up hitting
back.

YOU WANT A RIDE?
NO.
YOU SURE?
YES.
DUI MEETINGS

Maybe your words don't match what you want - like saying no while nodding your head yes.

This is a great way to avoid owning your position and dodge the feedback.

HI! I'D LIKE A RIDE.
RPW555

THE BEGINNING OF A MEANINGFUL, CODEPENDENT RELATIONSHIP.

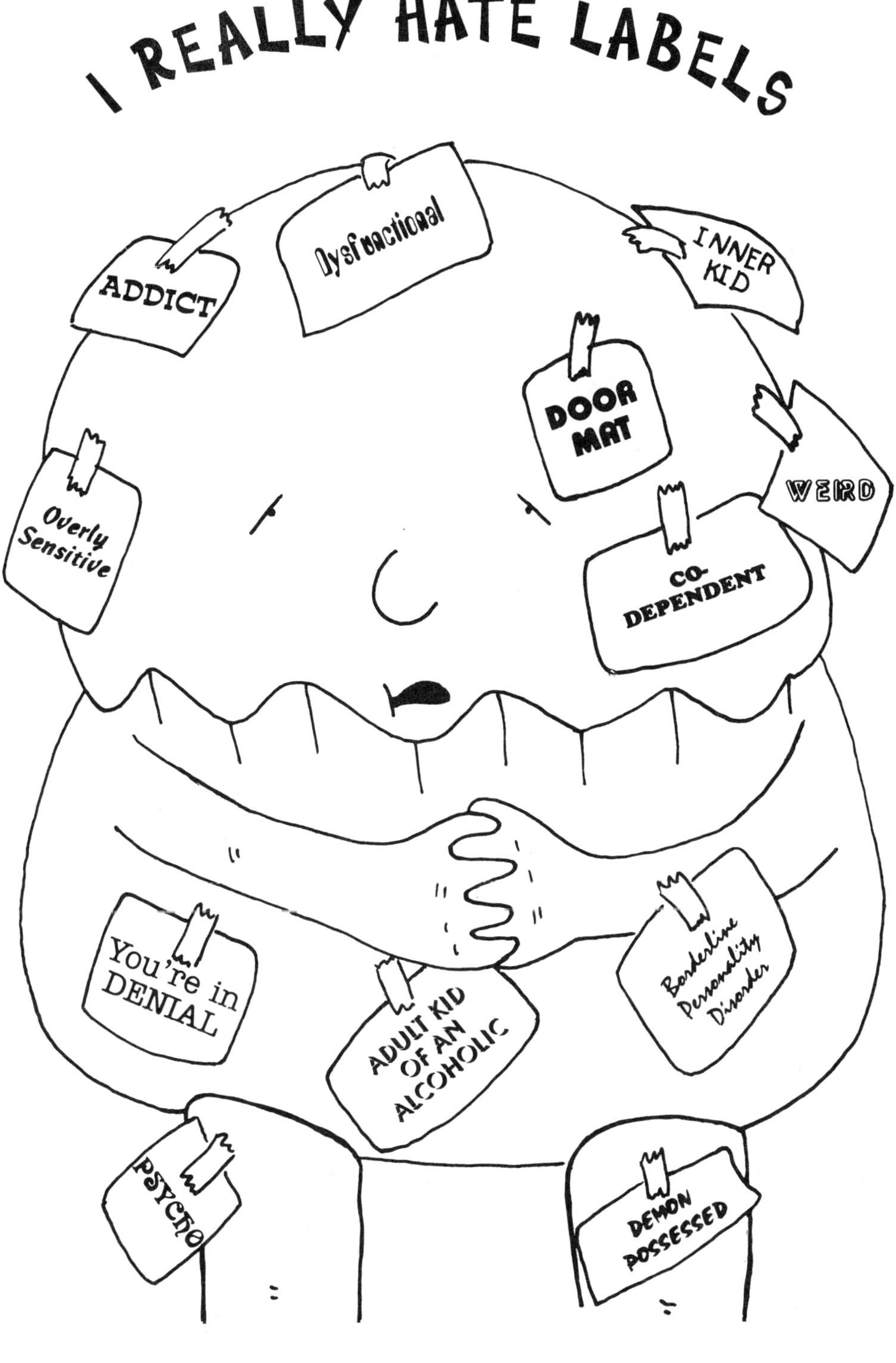
I REALLY HATE LABELS
ADDICT
Dysfunctional
INNER KID
DOOR MAT
WEIRD
Overly Sensitive
CO-DEPENDENT
You're in DENIAL
ADULT KID OF AN ALCOHOLIC
Borderline Personality Disorder
PSYCHO
DEMON POSSESSED

A FEW DAYS LATER . . .

I ONLY CAME TO HELP MY NEPHEW WHO DRINKS. I'VE TRIED EVERYTHING, I MEAN, I'VE LOST WEIGHT OVER HIM.
PRIVATE BEACH BELOW BEANS ONLY
I SUGGEST IT'S TIME TO TAKE CARE OF YOU. START ATTENDING CO-DEPENDENCY MEETINGS, AND LET SOMEONE ELSE TAKE OVER FOR YOU. HAVE A GOOD DAY!

TIME TO TAKE CARE OF ME?
CODEPENDENCY?
WHAT A RIDICULOUS IDEA!
ANYWAY, I REALLY HATE LABELS.

What do you carry

when you shoulder

another's burdens -

a bag over your head,
a sack of potatoes under
your arm,
a spare tire round your
middle,
and corns on your feet.

It's pretty hard to have the

energy to do your own thing.

PEARLS OF WISDOM

HMMM.......GREAT SMELL.
WHAT IS IT, AHHH...........BEANS?
..........BAKED BEANS?
PRIVATE BEACH
BELOW
BEANS ONLY

NEXT DAY
WATCH YOURSELF. EVERYONE WHO GOT CLOSE TO HER DISAPPEARED.
MYSTERY THEATER PRESENTS
ACME ERASER
click!

HOW COULD THAT COUNSELOR KICK ME OUT OF HIS DUI GROUP! I FEEL SO.................SO....
TUNE IN TOMORRROW AND FIND OUT IF CATHY COOKIE CUTTER GETS HER WAY, ONE MORE TIME!
click!

I'VE SPENT SO MUCH OF MY LIFE HELPING OTHERS... AND THIS IS THE THANKS I GET!
I FEEL SO..........SO..........
click!

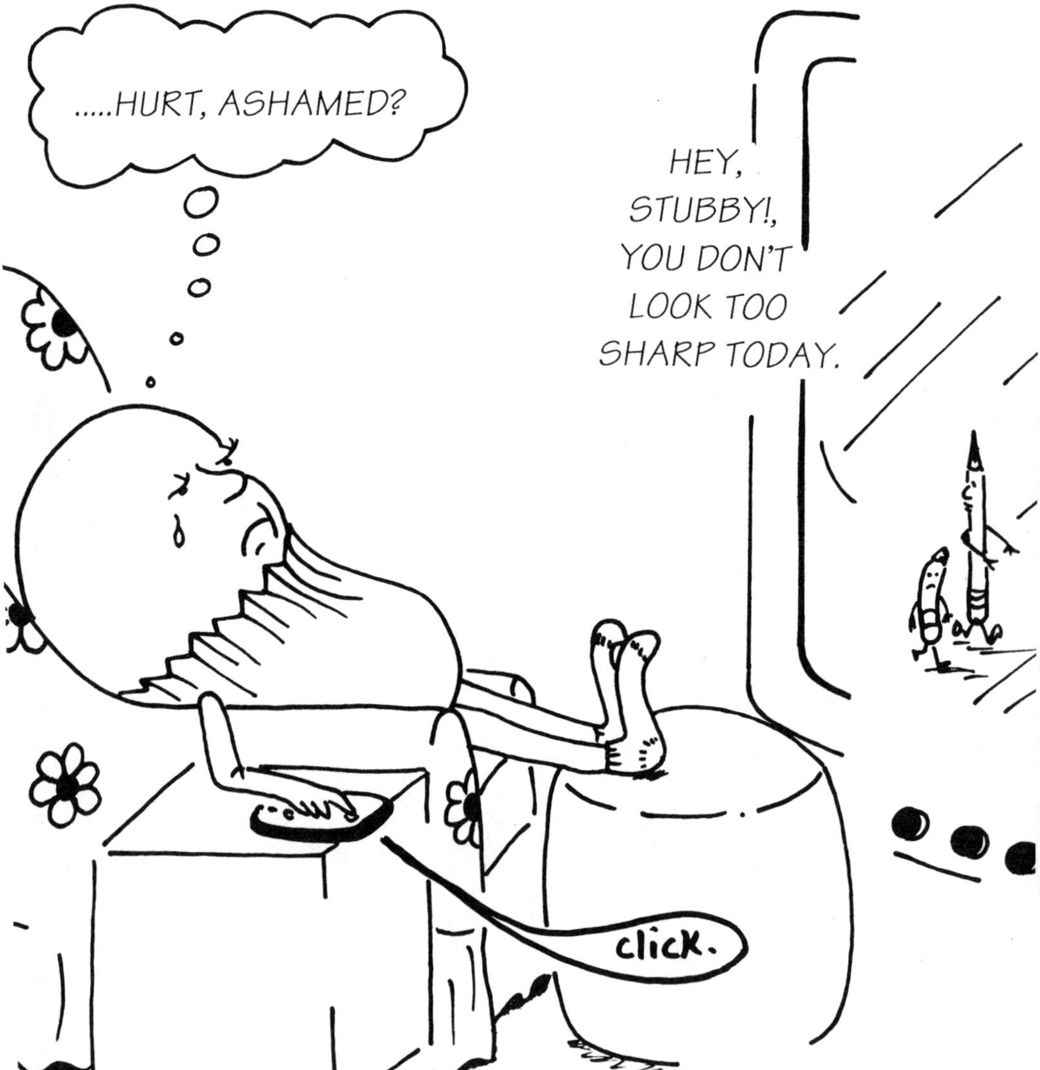
.....HURT, ASHAMED?
HEY, STUBBY!, YOU DON'T LOOK TOO SHARP TODAY.
click.

Depression; small bits of memory
which say we're not good enough,
and create reactions to what we
perceive is happening now -

and expand to overwhelming
proportions.

Know, then, that the child's
life events were each
profoundly powerful.

WELL, I SUPPOSE I SHOULD GO TO THE LIBRARY AND CHECK OUT SOME BOOKS ON CODEPENDENCY. ....SIGH.
click.

I WILL NOT

SHOULD ON MYSELF

TODAY

TOMORROW, MAYBE. . .

LATER...
QUIET
SELF HELP
"MANY CODEPENDENTS SEEM TO ATTRACT PEOPLE WITH PROBLEMS. THEY TAKE OVER OTHERS' RESPONSIBILITIES AND CALL THEM THEIR OWN, AND WHEN THINGS DON'T WORK OUT, THEY GET TO FEEL SORRY FOR THEMSELVES.... HOW COULD THEY DO THIS TO ME?"

QUIET
SELF HELP
NOT!

We don't like the unknown.

We prefer to be right -

Even if we're wrong.

C.C.'S INNER KID

"PURCHASE A DOLL, AND TREAT IT AS YOU WOULD LIKED TO HAVE BEEN TREATED AS A CHILD. TAKE THIS DOLL - YOUR **INNER CHILD** - WITH YOU EVERYWHERE. LET HER KNOW YOU'LL BE THERE FOR HER FOREVER AND EVER...."
NOW THIS IS MORE LIKE IT!
SELF HELP
QUIET
MORE SELF HELP
INNER KID
CO-DEPENDENT NO MORE
Codependent FOREVER

14.00
18.50
20.00
12.50

AN ADULT WITH A DOLL -
REALLY!
A DOLL?
Special Crackers

Being aware of how you

grew up tells you how

little you are in your

profoundest beliefs.

In knowing this
(how little you are),

you discover how big your

power is to adjust your
life.

Cheesos
Chee
Cheeso
Chees
Cheesos

ANDREA? - LET'S DO LUNCH!
THERE'S SOMEONE I WANT YOU
TO MEET ....NO, IT'S A SURPRISE.

A DOLL ?

ANDREA, I'D LIKE YOU TO MEET
MY INNER CHILD.
UH, HUH, OKAY,...SURE.

YES, AND YOU HAVE ONE, TOO.
ONE WHAT?

YOUR OWN INNER CHILD, SILLY.
NO KIDDING!
AND ALL I HAVE TO DO IS BUY
A DOLL AND TAKE IT TO LUNCH?

DO YOU THINK I SHOULD
ASK FOR A BOOSTER CHAIR?

WAITER! MY LITTLE FRIEND
WOULD LIKE A BOOSTER CHAIR.

NOW, WOULD YOUR LITTLE
FRIEND LIKE TO ORDER, TOO?
NO, DOLLS DON'T EAT, SILLY.

Those who don't believe

in elves may be our

most practical people.

They are also the ones

who stay hooked up

to the systems'

life-support machines.

FRIENDSHIPS ARE LIKE A PUZZLE

A COUPLE WEEKS LATER . . .

PETER PICKLE?
BEFORE I PICK YOU
UP FOR YOUR FIFTH
DUI MEETING, I WANT
TO ASK YOU TO COME WITH
ME TO AN ALL DAY SEMINAR
THIS SATURDAY. SOME OF
IT IS ABOUT POSITIVE
THINKING, AND GOD
KNOWS YOU NEED IT.

HELLO? . . . . HELLOOOOO

UH HUH, UH HUH. SO YOU'RE
FEELING PRESSURED . . . I
THINK YOU'RE RESISTING.
AND I DON'T WANT THIS
RELATIONSHIP TO BE A ONE
WAY STREET, WHERE I GIVE,
AND YOU TAKE. YA KNOW,
IT SHOULD WORK BOTH WAYS.

...GREAT! GOOD!
I'LL PICK YOU UP
IN HALF AN HOUR.

Friendships are like a puzzle -
they take time to figure out.

Don't overlook the pieces that
tell you what you may ask for -
and what you have to give -
to be a friend,
to have a friend.

SO... WHO'S THE DOLL,
AND WHY SO TENSE?
MY INNER CHILD, AND
I FORGOT MY GLASSES.

WHAT? WHAT? YOU FORGOT YOUR GLASSES? YOU TOLD ME YOU CAN'T DRIVE WITH-OUT THEM!
DON'T TALK TO ME! I HAVE TO CONCENTRATE.

LOOK OUT!
A PEDESTRIAN!
A PEDESTRIAN!

GOD, JUST LET ME HAVE MY LICENSE BACK, AND I WILL NEVER, EVER, DRINK AND DRIVE AGAIN.
DUI MEETINGS

If your knees are shaky,
maybe you've been scared.

Your body may also be
telling you
you need to talk about something.

THE SEMINAR

WELL, PETER, WHAT PART OF THE SEMINAR DO YOU THINK YOU'LL LIKE BEST?
LUNCH.

HEY, THERE, GUYS & GALS. I'M DR. SPUD PIENSKY. LIFE IS WHAT YOU MAKE IT! THE SKY'S THE LIMIT!
Cookie
WHY, PEACE IS BREAKING OUT ALL OVER. THE BERLIN WALL'S DOWN . . . THE RUSSIANS ARE NO LONGER OUR ENEMY . . . . EASTERN EUROPE IS FREE!
Hmmmmm . . . RWANDA . . . BOSNIA . . . DESERT STORM . . . . HAITI . . . NORTH KOREA . . . RUSSIAN MAFIA . . . AK-47s.
Cookie

WE'RE LIVING IN AN INCREDIBLE AGE. GREAT THINGS ARE HAPPENING. BUT -- IF YOU GET A LEMON, MAKE LEMONADE.
GIVE ME A BREAK.
Cookie
YES, GREAT! BE POSITIVE! GET OFF THE PITY POT, AND GET WITH THE PROGRAM. LIFE'S FUN! IF YOU FEEL LIKE DUNG, IT'S YOUR FAULT. SO STOP THAT NEGATIVE SELF-TALK AND LEARN TO LOVE YOURSELF . . . JUST IN CASE NO ONE ELSE DOES. BLAH, BLAH . . . .
Cookie
TERRIFYING. ABSOLUTELY TERRIFYING.

LUNCH BREAK

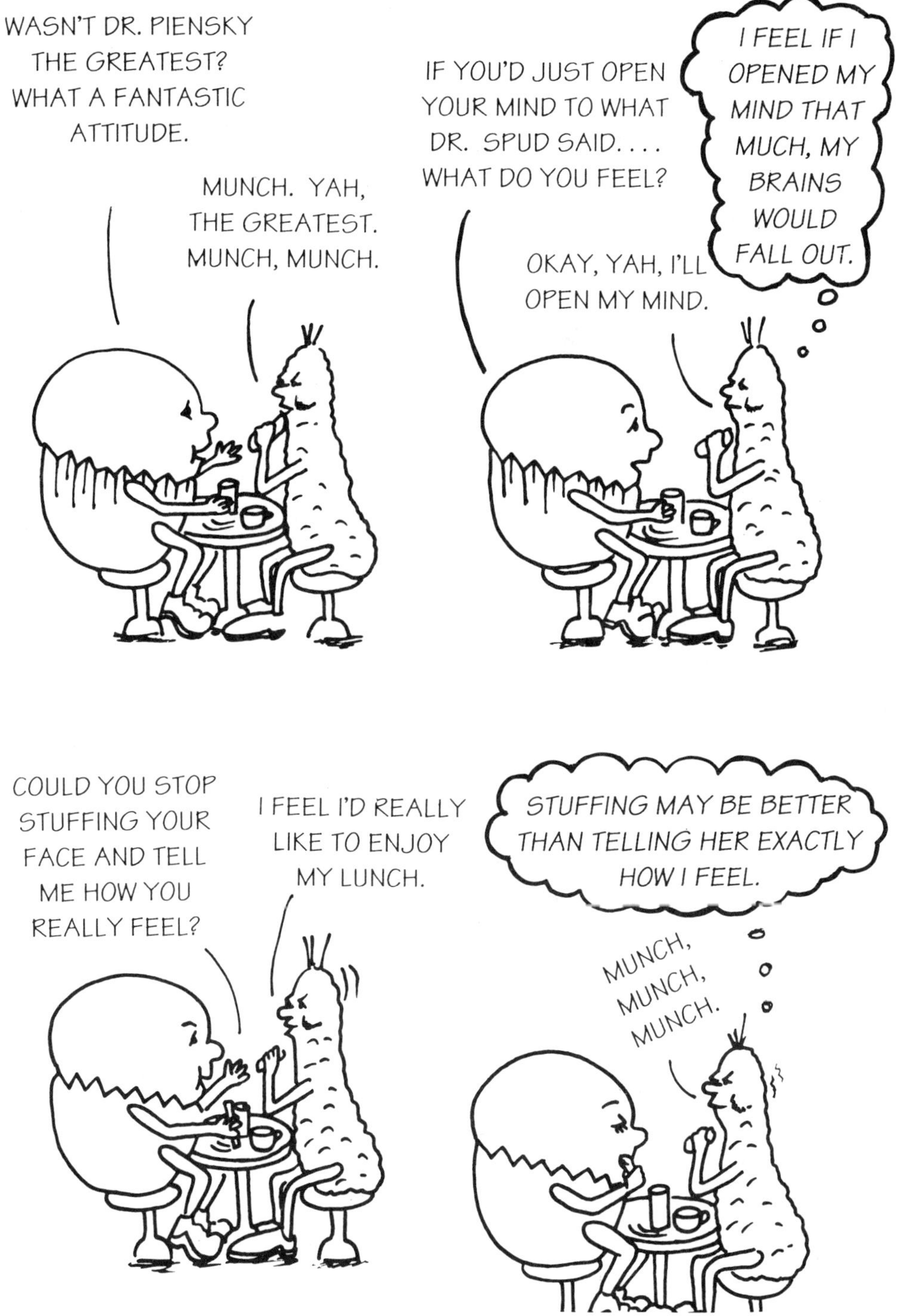
WASN'T DR. PIENSKY THE GREATEST? WHAT A FANTASTIC ATTITUDE.
MUNCH. YAH, THE GREATEST. MUNCH, MUNCH.
IF YOU'D JUST OPEN YOUR MIND TO WHAT DR. SPUD SAID. . . . WHAT DO YOU FEEL?
OKAY, YAH, I'LL OPEN MY MIND.
I FEEL IF I OPENED MY MIND THAT MUCH, MY BRAINS WOULD FALL OUT.
COULD YOU STOP STUFFING YOUR FACE AND TELL ME HOW YOU REALLY FEEL?
I FEEL I'D REALLY LIKE TO ENJOY MY LUNCH.
STUFFING MAY BE BETTER THAN TELLING HER EXACTLY HOW I FEEL.
MUNCH, MUNCH, MUNCH.

LAST SESSION OF THE DAY

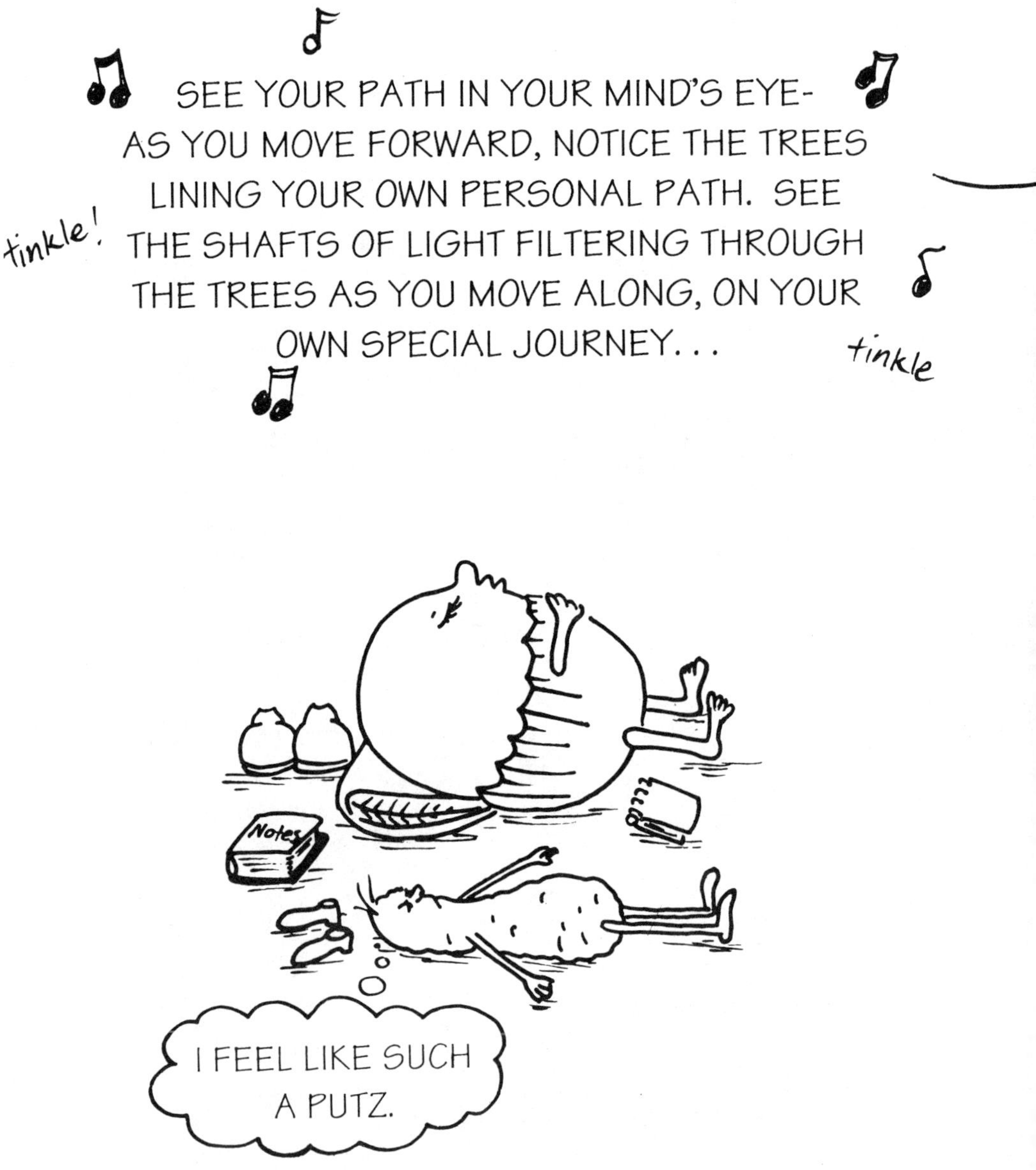

NOTICE HOW THE WATER LAPS AT YOUR FEET, AS YOU STROLL ON YOUR PRIVATE BEACH.
tinkle!
Notes
I CAN THINK OF A DOZEN WAYS I'D RATHER TAKE A TRIP. CHEAPER, TOO.

LEAVING NOW, COMING BACK,
FEELING FINE . . . FEELING
REFRESHED.

BREAK INTO GROUPS OF FIVE,
AND SHARE YOUR JOURNEY'S
EXPERIENCE.

AND THE WATER PARTED SO I COULD GET TO THE OTHER SIDE, WHERE A PURPLE ELF, ON A LAVENDER TOADSTOOL, SAT WAITING FOR ME.
REALLY?
GIVE ME A BREAK.

When you think others have acted foolishly, give them at least one pat on the back for their willingness to expose themselves.

They may have gained a new way of acting by fooling their rigid beliefs about how they SHOULD perform.

WELL, PETER, WHAT
PART OF THE SEMINAR
DID YOU LIKE BEST?
LUNCH!

When we get into one routine

or program only, we act as if

there is nothing more to do.

Why?

I STILL THINK THAT BIT ABOUT THE PURPLE ELF WAS PRETTY WEIRD.
UH HUH. I WANT YOU TO COME OVER FRIDAY NIGHT, 'CUZ' I HAVE A SURPRISE FOR YOU.

I KNEW IT! SHE LIKES ME.
SHE REALLY LIKES ME.
OKAY

EXPECTATIONS
PUTT!
....Sputter..
.....Sputter....
Sighhhh...

FRIDAY EVENING

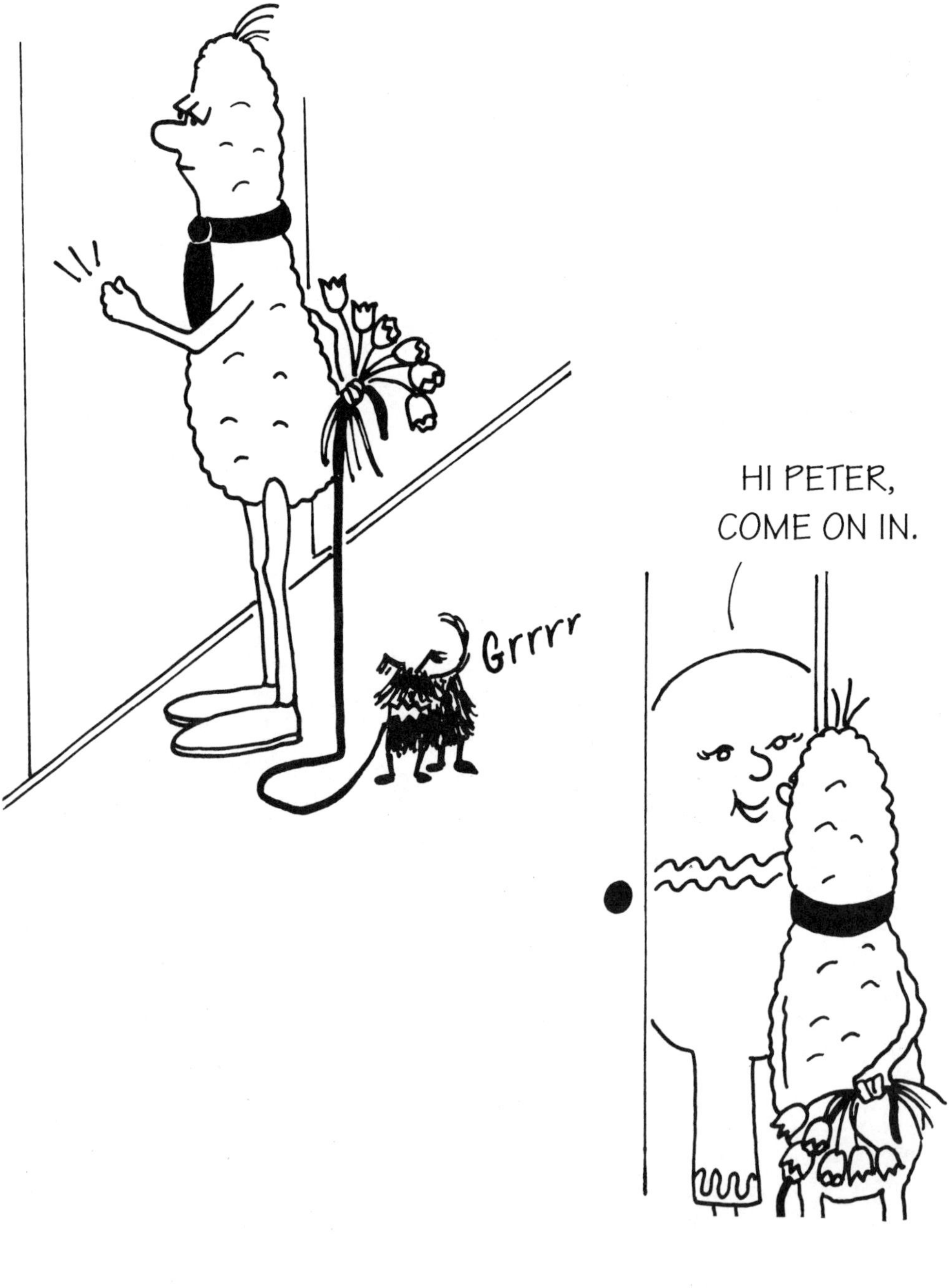

A DOG, YOU BOUGHT
ME A DOG?

BUT YOU TOLD ME
YOU LOVED DOGS.

THAT DIDN'T MEAN
I WANTED ONE.

AHH . . . . BUT . . . .

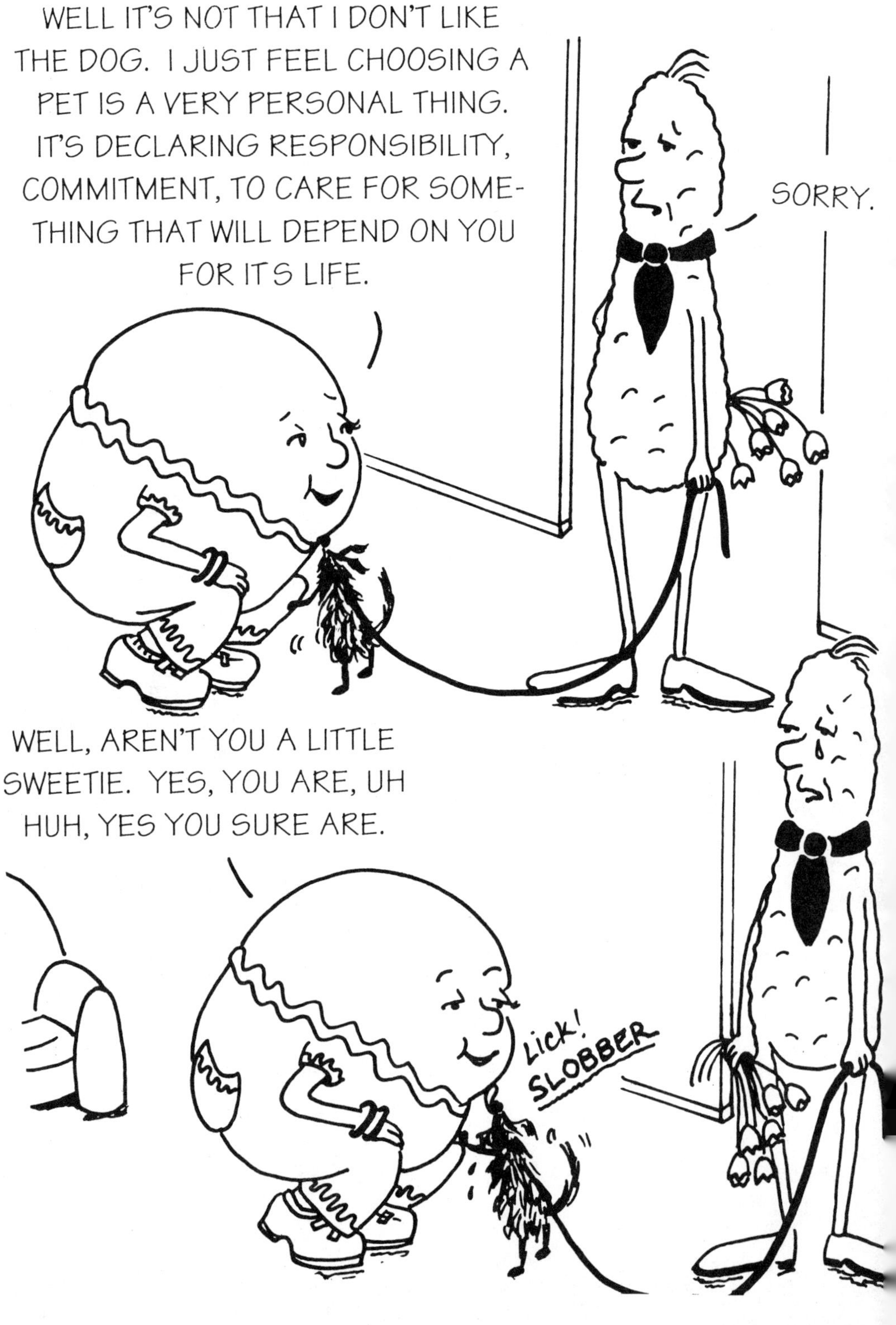
WELL IT'S NOT THAT I DON'T LIKE THE DOG. I JUST FEEL CHOOSING A PET IS A VERY PERSONAL THING. IT'S DECLARING RESPONSIBILITY, COMMITMENT, TO CARE FOR SOME-THING THAT WILL DEPEND ON YOU FOR ITS LIFE.
SORRY.
WELL, AREN'T YOU A LITTLE SWEETIE. YES, YOU ARE, UH HUH, YES YOU SURE ARE.
LICK!
SLOBBER

ARE YOU OKAY?
I'M SORRY, PETER.
I'M LEAVING NOW.
I REALLY LOVE THE DOG.
I WAS JUST SO SURPRISED.
FORGIVE ME?

PLEASE, PLEASE STAY.
WELL, AT LEAST LET ME GIVE YOU YOUR SURPRISE. I'VE BEEN SO EXCITED JUST THINKING OF GIVING IT TO YOU. I'LL BE RIGHT BACK.
I'M STILL LEAVING NOW.
OKAY.
WELL, I GUESS I COULD FORGIVE HER.

HERE YA' GO. A BRAND NEW VIDEO ON BURIED RESENTMENT AND THE ADDICTIVE PERSONALITY.
THANKS.
Video
I **REALLLEEE** HATE HER!
REALLLEEE LOVE THE DOOOGEEE.
I'LL PICK YOU UP FOR YOUR MEETING TUES-DAY. LOVE THE FLOWERS! **BYE BYYYEE!**
I BET HE REALLLEEE HATES ME.

When you avoid your need to confront

(directly or from a safe distance) -

you nurture fear.

When you don't want to care anymore -

you're giving up on your desires.

STOP IT, SILLY.
I WANT TO INTRODUCE
YOU TO TAO.

THIS IS MY CAT, TAO.
A TRAIN COULD COME THROUGH HERE AND
SHE'D NEVER MOVE
A MUSCLE.
GRRRRRR
RUFF!

ZOOM!
WELL, SO MUCH
FOR THAT THEORY.

SMOOTHING RUFFLED FEATHERS

MONDAY A.M., AT WORK

NO, I WORKED IT OUT.
DO YOU MIND STOPPING BY ON YOUR LUNCH BREAK AND TAKING ME TO THE RECYCLING STATION?
Foot going!
jiggle
Cola
Diet Cola
Mariners

YES, OF COURSE, THAT'S THE LEAST I CAN DO. . . EVEN THOUGH I ONLY HAVE HALF AN HOUR FOR LUNCH.
MS. CUPCAKE, ADM. ASST.

BOY, HE'S GOT SOME NERVE!
SLAM!
MS. CUPCAKE, ADM. ASST.

AS YOUR SUPERVISOR,
I EXPECT YOU TO KEEP
AN EYE ON THE PENNY PINCHING.
Zip
MS. CUPCAKE, ADM. ASST.

AS UPPER MANAGEMENT, ISN'T THAT YOUR JOB? I MEAN, WELL, I'VE HEARD THAT A LOT OF OUR EMPLOYEES ARE GOING TO BE LET GO. . . . WON'T THAT HELP YOUR PENNY PINCHING?

NOT THAT.
"THAT!"
Pinch
One Cent
10¢
Whip!
BURRITO ROLL
MS. CUPCAKE, ADM. ASST.

JUST FOR YOUR INFORMATION, WE AREN'T LETTING GO OF ANY OF OUR EMPLOYEES. IT'S CALLED DOWN-SIZING. SPEAKING AS UPPER MANAGEMENT, WE INTEND TO TELL THEM THE SAME DAY THEY ARE TO LEAVE, BECAUSE WE DON'T WANT TO UPSET THEM AHEAD OF TIME, WHICH WOULD INTERFERE WITH THEIR WORK FLOW.
OR THE FACT THEY NO LONGER HAVE ONE.

LIKE THE DOG?
LOVE THE DOG.
HE NEEDS HIS SHOTS.
OH, BROTHER.
WATCH THE CURB!

WHY DO YOU DRINK SO MUCH DIET COLA?
CUZ' I LIKE IT?
WHAT CURB?

CLUNK
BONK
BAM!
CLANK
REALITY CHECK. . .
HOW DID YOU EVER
PASS A DRIVER'S TEST?
DIDN'T.
GOTTA LICENSE.
WHAT?
YOU DON'T HAVE A LICENSE?

WHEN I WAS FIFTEEN I GOT A DRIVER'S PERMIT. BUT BEING A CITY GIRL, I JUST CONTINUED TAKING THE BUS. I USED MY PERMIT FOR IDENTIFICATION, SO I HAD TO UPDATE WITH A NEW PICTURE EVERY FEW YEARS. WELL, WHAT CAN I SAY . . . YOU KNOW HOW LONG THOSE LINES ARE AT THE DMV- THEY'RE OVERCROWDED AND UNDER-STAFFED. SO WHEN THIS GUY GOT TO ME, HE MUST HAVE BEEN PRETTY TIRED, CUZ' WHEN I GAVE HIM MY PERMIT, HE GAVE ME BACK A LICENSE.

PRETTY NEAT, HUH.

TATER'S
BAG
OF
TROUBLES

WHY DIDN'T YOU TAKE ADVANTAGE OF THE LIST OF MEETINGS I GAVE YOUR MOTHER?
I REALIZE IT'S HARD BEING SIXTEEN, ESPECIALLY IN THESE TIMES, AND, OF COURSE, YOUR DAD'S DRINKING. BUT THERE COMES A TIME WHEN YOU MUST STAND UP AND TAKE RESPONSIBILITY FOR YOUR ACTIONS. YOU, NOT YOUR PARENTS, WRAPPED YOUR MOTHER'S NEW CAR AROUND A TREE. NO ONE HELD YOU DOWN AND FORCED ALCOHOL AND DRUGS DOWN YOUR THROAT. YOU DID THAT. ARE YOU GOING TO FACE YOUR FEELNGS, YOUR PROBLEMS, OR KEEP SCREWING UP?
DON'T KNOW.
AUNT C.C., I REALLY HATE IT WHEN YOU LECTURE ME.

LECTURE? ME LECTURE YOU? HOW RIDICULOUS. LISTEN TO ME, TATER, I'M ONLY TRYING TO GIVE YOU SOME OF MY YEARS OF LIVING EXPERIENCE, MY WISDOM. BUT IF YOU FEEL I'M LECTURING YOU, I'LL TAKE A DIFFERENT APPROACH BY TELLING YOU A TRUE STORY ABOUT A MOUSE NAMED JELLY BEAN, WHO WAS GAMBLING AWAY HIS FAMILY'S FORTUNE. HE FELT JUST AWFUL, BUT CONTINUED HIS ADDICTION.

THEN HIS CHILDREN, MOTHER, WIFE, AND A COUNSELOR CONFRONTED HIM. I THINK IT WAS CALLED INTERVENTION. ANYWAY, TO MAKE A LONG STORY SHORT, HE QUIT GAMBLING AND TRIED TO KEEP HIS FEELINGS, HIS TROUBLES, BURIED.

TROUBLE AREA
Troubles
Troubles
TAP
TAP
TAP
BUT THEN, ...

HE STARTED DRINKING A LOT, AND THE WIFE AND KIDS LEFT. SO TO GET THEM BACK, HE WENT TO A 12 STEP PROGRAM AND GOT "DRY", NOT "SOBER", BECAUSE HIS PROBLEMS WERE STILL BURIED AND HE FELT REALLY UNCOMFORTABLE.

HIS NEXT ADDICTION WAS WORKING TOO HARD, A WORKAHOLIC, WHICH EVERYONE JUST LOVED. JELLY BEAN WAS MAKING LOTS OF MONEY, HE CAME HOME EVERY EVENING, AND THEY MOVED TO AN UPSCALE NEIGHBORHOOD. SOON HE WAS INTO OVERTIME, TIME AND A HALF, DOUBLE TIME, AND HIS FAMILY BECAME VERY LONELY WITHOUT HIM. THEN THE COMPUTER AT WORK WASN'T ENOUGH, SO HE BOUGHT ANOTHER HE COULD USE AT HOME TO FILL UP THE REST OF HIS LIFE. WITH VERY LITTLE SLEEP, HE STARTED TO HALLUCINATE, AND HIS WIFE TURNED TO THEIR CHILDREN TO GET HER EMOTIONAL NEEDS MET - BUT THAT'S A WHOLE OTHER STORY. WORKAHOLISM IS ALMOST THE HARDEST ADDICTION TO ACCEPT BECAUSE EVERYONE AND SOCIETY APPLAUDS PEOPLE WHO WORK SO HARD. WELL, ANYWAY, WHERE WAS I? OH YES,..... THEN ONE DAY, A SMALL THING HAPPENED, BUT WE DON'T KNOW WHAT MIGHT BE THE ONE EXPERIENCE THAT TRIGGERS POSITIVE CHANGE. JELLY BEAN WENT TO THE BOOKSTORE TO BUY THE UPDATED COMPUTER BOOK OF HIS DREAMS. HE WAS SO EXCITED THAT HE RUSHED DOWN THE WRONG AISLE, STOPPED, REACHED OUT, AND GRABBED A BOOK TITLED, ***DEAL WITH IT***. JELLY BEAN STARTED TO READ...

CAUTION:
BURYING TROUBLES
CAN BE HAZARDOUS
TO YOUR HEALTH.
BEST TO BRING
TROUBLES OUT
INTO THE OPEN.
SELF HELP
QUIET
Deal With IT
TROUBLE AREA
Troubles
OPEN AREA
Troubles
PAT
PAT
PAT!
Troubles

NOW, TATER, YOU REALLY DON'T WANT TO GO THROUGH ALL THAT, DO YOU? OF COURSE NOT. SO THE SOONER YOU FACE UP TO YOUR TROUBLES, THE BETTER CHANCE FOR A NORMAL LIFE YOU'LL HAVE.
O.K., AUNT C.C. I WILL! TRUST ME.
YA, SURE, YA BET. HEH, HEH, HEH.
GOOD, BECAUSE I ENROLLED YOU IN A YOUTH PROGRAM IN YAKIMA. A LOCK DOWN FACILITY, SO YOU CAN'T WALK OFF THIS TIME. LET'S GO.

THAT WAS A REALLY GREAT CONVERSATION WE HAD . . . . DON'T YOU THINK?

SETTING BOUNDARIES

I'M A SETTIN' A BOUNDARY, PARDNER. CROSS THAT LINE AND I'LL PLUG YA!
BUT WHO WILL TAKE CARE OF ME? I DON'T KNOW HOW TO SURVIVE WITHOUT YOU. I WON'T HAVE ANYONE TO BLAME FOR MY MISTAKES, MY LIFE!

SYMPTOMS: HARD TIME ASKING FOR WHAT THEY WANT OR NEED; CAN'T SET LIMITS ON OTHERS' BEHAVIORS, E.G., THAT'S ENOUGH, DON'T DO THAT.
WHAT DO YOU MEAN, ANDREA, I'M NOT LISTENING . . . YOUR BROTHER STOLE YOUR CAR, AND YOU LOST YOUR JOB.
SYMPTOM: DIFFICULTY RECOGNIZING WHAT'S ABUSIVE OR DANGEROUS TO THEM.
Setting BOUNDARIES
UH HUH, UH HUH, YES ANDREA, I SEE. REALLY . . . UH HUH.
ZZZ

If you give up your space
defined by boundaries
which state this is where
I begin and you end -

you'll have to learn how
to be a chameleon.

Remember: If you let
others draw them for
you, they can change
them at any time....

YOUR DOG HAVE A PROBLEM WITH BOUNDARIES?
NO, JUST PORCUPINES
Alpine View VETERINARY CLINIC
WHAT'S A BOUNDARY?
GRRR
WELL, I GUESS IN THIS CASE A BOUNDARY IS AN INVISIBLE SPACE THAT'S HIS AND NO ONE ELSE'S
SOUNDS LIKE SOMETHING I COULD USE. I'M ALWAYS GETTING TALKED INTO SOMETHING OR OTHER, IT SEEMS.
Alpine View VETERINARY CLINIC

WELL, I DON'T KNOW YOU, BUT I'M GOING TO A DANCE THERAPY TUESDAY NIGHT. I THINK SOME OF IT HAS TO DO WITH LEARNING TO DEFINE YOUR SPACE AND CLAIMING IT AS YOUR OWN. DO YOU WANT TO GO?
GREAT. I'D LOVE TO. AND YOU'LL PICK ME UP, RIGHT?

WOW, I'LL BRING MY FRIEND. HER HUS-BAND JUST LEFT HER ... MAYBE YOU CAN HELP HER. SHE HAS LOTS OF PROBLEMS. I JUST KNOW YOU'LL LOVE HER.

I LIVE IN LYNNWOOD, NOT TOO FAR, IS IT? HUH? HUH?
WHY DO I ALWAYS DO THIS?

WELL, BACK TO THE DRAWING TABLE.

DANCE THERAPY

GOOD EVENING, AND WELCOME TO DANCE THERAPY. PLEASE SHOW ME THE SPACE YOU'LL ALLOW YOURSELF TO MOVE IN.
HOW EXCITING!
OH BOY, OH BOY!

HI. I'M SPECIAL, AND YOU'RE NOT!
I WANT THE WHOLE FLOOR.
NO PROBLEM.
HERE'S MY SPACE.
I WANT THIS CORNER.

If you want to avoid conflict

within your own self,

and over what you want

to be -

you create an arena

in which you must win.

And this is how you treat others.

TAP
TAP!

SURPRISE!
ZAP!
TAP!

If you find you
receive pleasure for
your needs and desires
by possessing
and controlling -

Wake up to the actions
of the person who
taught you this
by receiving pleasure
from possessing and
controlling you.

TA DA!
MR. EGGPLANT, THIS IS DEFINITELY NOT APPROPRIATE BEHAVIOR.
WHAP!

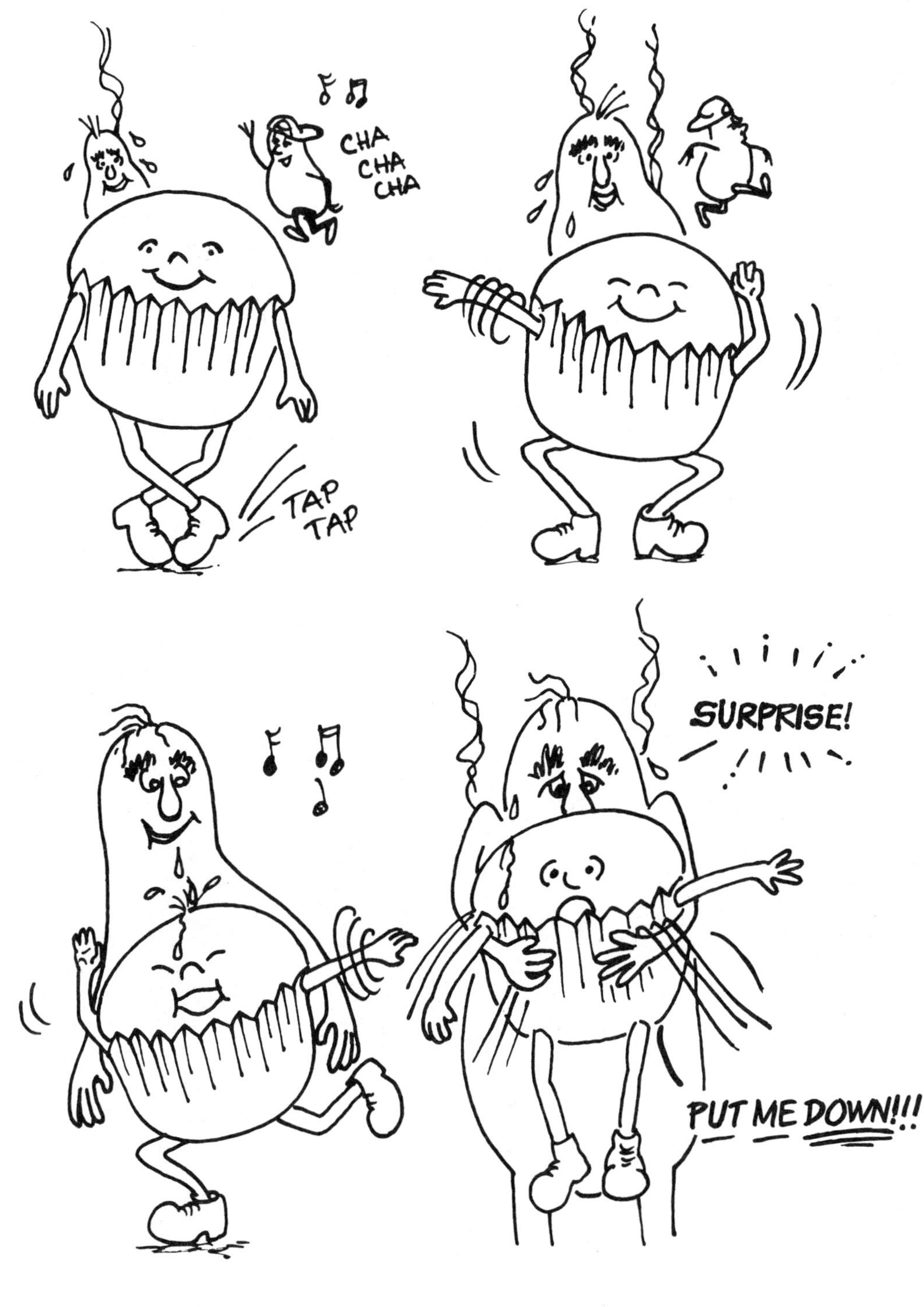
CHA
CHA
CHA
TAP
TAP
SURPRISE!
PUT ME DOWN!!!

AHH, COME ON.
NO.
WHY?
JUST DON'T WANT TO.
COME ON,
I WON'T HURT YOU.
NO, I DON'T WANT TO.
PLEASE,
PLEASE,
PLEASE.
HE'S SLIMY, STINKS,
AND IS UGLY.
NO!!!

When you continue to submit -
you're empowering your
powerlessness.

When you allow another's opinion
preeminence over your view
of reality -
you're permitting yourself
to be a victim of seduction.

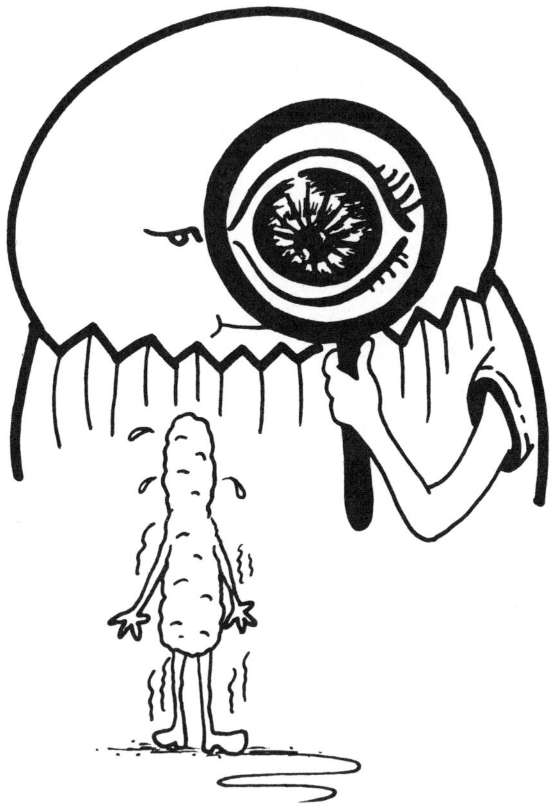

GETTING TO KNOW YOU

RAINY DAY LUNCH

UMM, THAT LOOKS GREAT, CHEESE AND EGGS.
REALLY? WELL I DID GET CAUGHT IN THE RAIN. . . I'LL JUST HAVE TO DROP INTO A BAKERY BEAUTY SHOP AND GET IT FLUFFED. HUMIDITY CHANGES MY SHAPE FROM TIME TO TIME.
I DON'T WANT TO FREAK YOU OUT C.C., BUT THERE'S A CRATER WHERE THE TOP OF YOUR HEAD USED TO BE.
OH. . . . THAT'S WHY YOUR LOOK CHANGES SO MUCH. AND HERE I THOUGHT THE GAL WHO DRAWS US COULDN'T MAKE UP HER MIND ON HOW YOU SHOULD LOOK.
YOU CAN STOP WRINGING YOUR HANDS NOW.
CHEESE

PETER, WHAT'S WRONG?
I FEEL MY LIFE IS GOING NOWHERE BUT DOWN. I'VE LOST EVERYTHING, AND WORKING FOR MY BROTHER'S CLEANING SERVICE JUST DOESN'T CUT IT.
CHEESE
OH, PETER, YOU SHOULDN'T FEEL SO BAD. AS YOUR AA GROUP SAYS, YOU'RE RIGHT WHERE YOU'RE SUP-POSED TO BE. THE UNIVERSE WORKS IN MYSTERIOUS WAYS, AND SOME-TIMES WE NEED A KICK IN THE BUTT TO GET US OUT OF OUR OLD RUTS SO WE CAN MOVE ONTO EVEN BIGGER AND BETTER THINGS.

SO, TELL ME PETER, WHAT EXACTLY WAS YOUR PROFESSION?
BANKER.... MUNCH, MUNCH.
CHEESE
YOU MEAN YOU SHOVED DIRT AROUND, UP AGAINST ROADSIDES?
NO. BANKER. AS IN BEVERLY HILLS BANKER. MUNCH, MUNCH.
CHEES

SHE'S SPEECHLESS. WHAT A RELIEF.
MUNCH, MUNCH.
CHEE
YOU'RE STILL GOING TO SEE THE CHANNELER WITH ME, AREN'T YOU?
IF YOU GET YOUR HEAD TOGETHER, I WILL.
YUP.

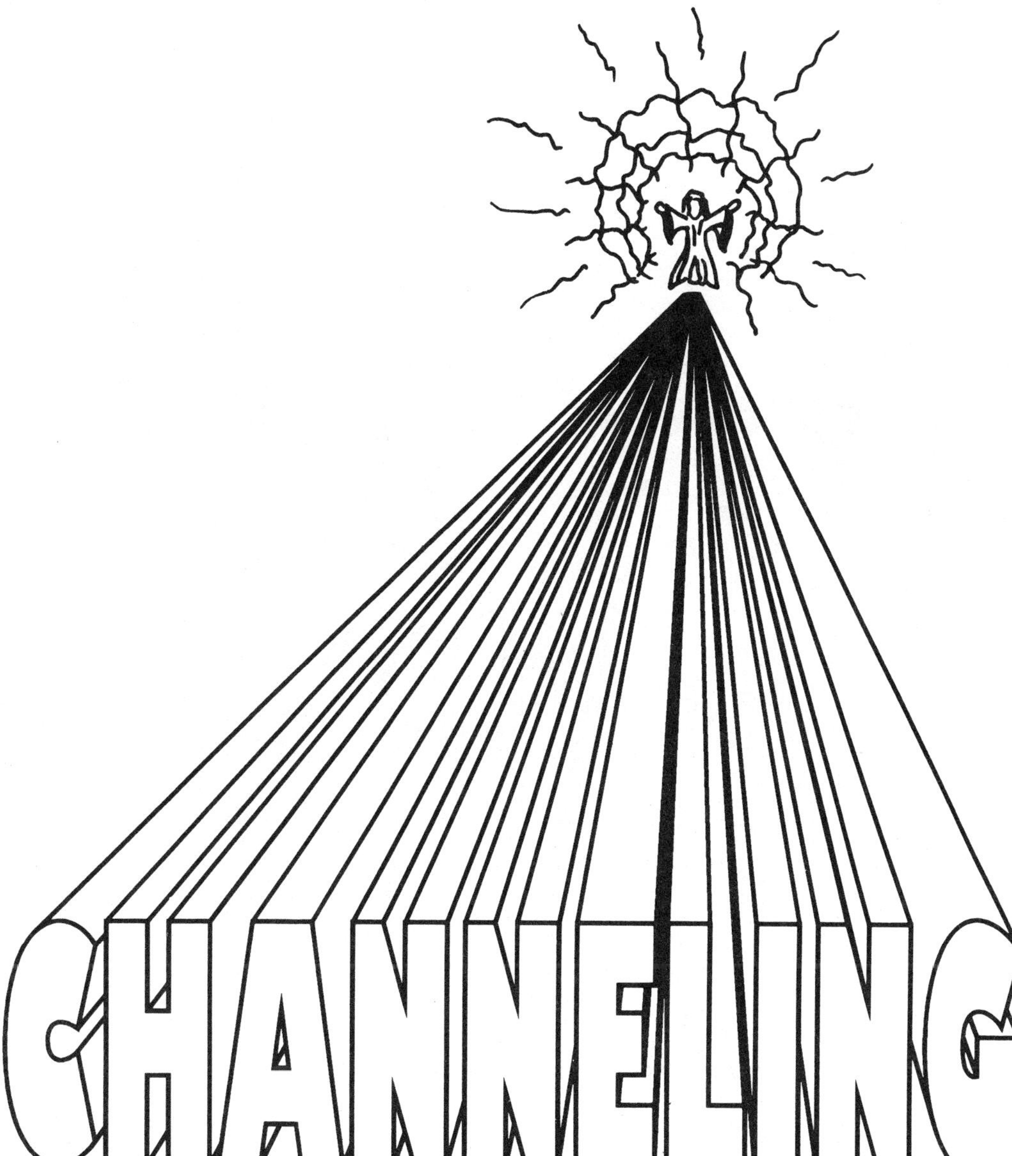
CHANNELING

NOW, LET ME GET THIS STRAIGHT. YOU'RE BACK-ING OUT BECAUSE . . . "IT'S ALL TOO WEIRD?"
YEAH, PLUS THERE ARE HUMANS ALL OVER THE PLACE.

YOU DON'T BOTHER THEM, THEY DON'T BOTHER YOU. IN FACT, HUMANS HAVE A PHENOMENAL DENIAL SYSTEM AND WILL ONLY SEE WHAT THEY WANT. BELIEVE ME, THE LAST THING THEY'D WANT TO ACKNOWLEDGE IS THAT WE ARE ON A PAR WITH THEM, INTELLECTUALLY, SPIRITUALLY, AND PHYSICALLY. . . . I MEAN, REALLY.
OKAY. I GIVE UP. YOU KNOW, C.C., YOU REALLY SHOULD RUN FOR OFFICE.

Whatever you resist, you feed.
We're afraid "it" or "they"
will win.

It's a funny thing about
surrender - when you don't
care anymore about who
wins, you're free to move
to another place.

An Awareness: It may feel
like you've really lost when
you first surrender. Go ahead
and allow how ugly and awful
that feels. Now that you've
endured the worst, you can
use the energy you put into
resisting to begin packing
your bags.

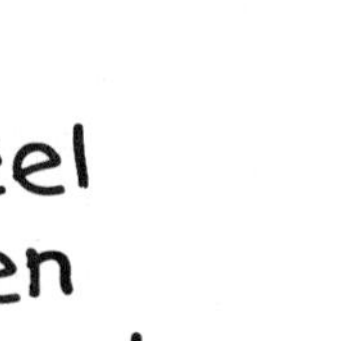

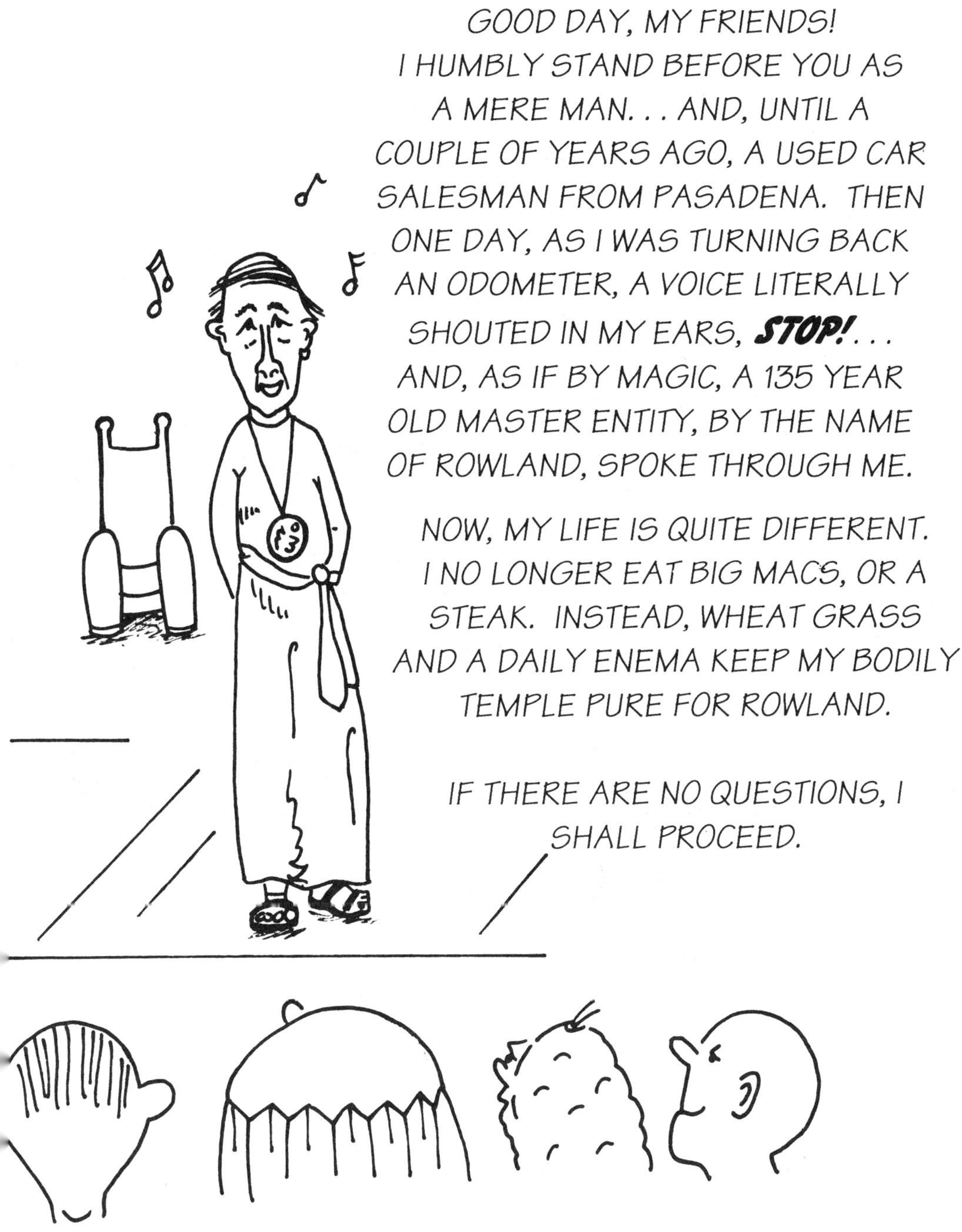
GOOD DAY, MY FRIENDS!
I HUMBLY STAND BEFORE YOU AS A MERE MAN. . . AND, UNTIL A COUPLE OF YEARS AGO, A USED CAR SALESMAN FROM PASADENA. THEN ONE DAY, AS I WAS TURNING BACK AN ODOMETER, A VOICE LITERALLY SHOUTED IN MY EARS, STOP!. . . AND, AS IF BY MAGIC, A 135 YEAR OLD MASTER ENTITY, BY THE NAME OF ROWLAND, SPOKE THROUGH ME.
NOW, MY LIFE IS QUITE DIFFERENT. I NO LONGER EAT BIG MACS, OR A STEAK. INSTEAD, WHEAT GRASS AND A DAILY ENEMA KEEP MY BODILY TEMPLE PURE FOR ROWLAND.
IF THERE ARE NO QUESTIONS, I SHALL PROCEED.

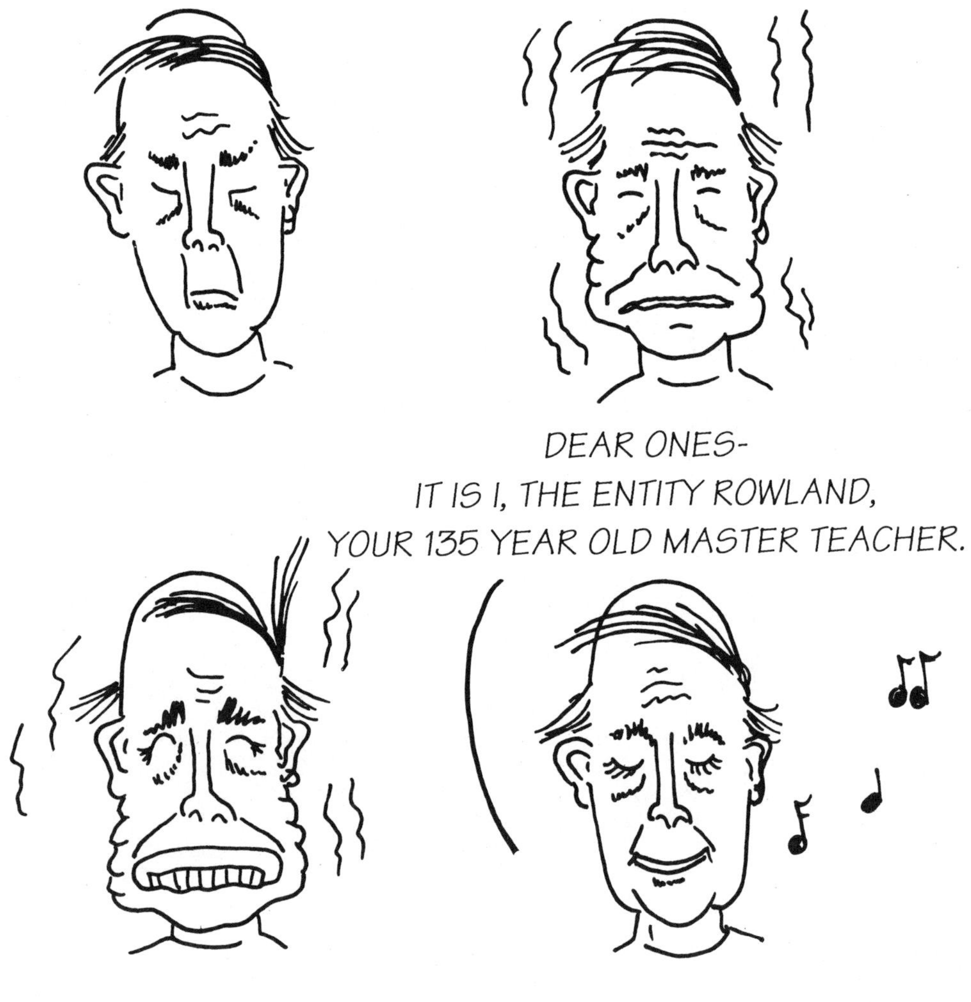
DEAR ONES-
IT IS I, THE ENTITY ROWLAND,
YOUR 135 YEAR OLD MASTER TEACHER.

NOW
SLAP!
HOLY SHAMOLY!

YOU ARE ALL ONE.
ONE IS YOU.
ONE AND ONE
MAKES TWO.
SO THERE IT IS!
SO BE IT!
AHHH!
OHHHHH
GIVE ME A BREAK!
WOW!

TWO HOURS LATER . . .

AND NOW, I WANT TO REMIND YOU THERE ARE ORDER TAKERS OUTSIDE THE DOORS FOR MY BOOKS AND TAPES ON WEIGHT LOSS, MONEY, LOVE, SUCCESS IN YOUR CAREER, GETTING WHAT YOU WANT ALL THE TIME, PAST LIVES, PARALLEL WORLDS, AND HOW TO CONTROL THE MYSTERIES OF THE UNIVERSE.

REMEMBER, TOO, THE RULE OF PROSPERITY: "YOU HAVE TO GIVE IN ORDER TO GET!"

WITH THAT, I'LL LEAVE, MY CHILDREN. BLESS YOU - IT IS A GOOD DAY TO TRANSCEND.

I DON'T KNOW IF THOSE WILL MAKE YOU HAPPY, BUT YOU'RE SURE MAKING OL' ROWLAND HAPPY. . . . RICH, TOO.
Hmmmm
Rowland's TRUTH

MAGIC, PETER, PLASTIC MAGIC.
HUMANS LOVE IT.
AND ANOTHER THING-
HOW CAN YOU AFFORD
ALL THIS.
VISA
Rowland's
TRUTH

Watch out for those
who say
this is the only way,
and if you don't
do as we do,
you'll never be able
to....

They're refusing to
see their own
further
possibilities,
or do the work
to uncover them.

THE VERY NEXT MORNING..

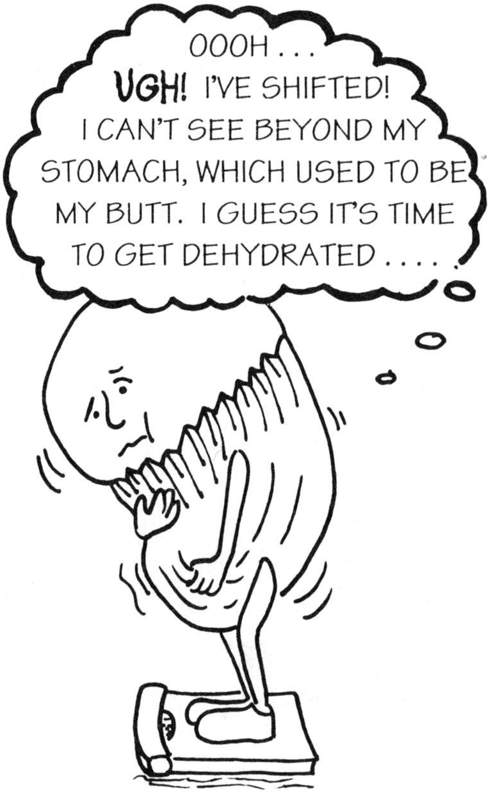

ANDREA? I MADE A DEHYDRATION APPOINTMENT FOR SATURDAY AT 8:00 A.M. I'M A LITTLE NERVOUS, SO I WANT YOU TO BE THERE FOR ME..... WHAT DO YOU MEAN, I SHOULDN'T DO IT. WHY?..... OF COURSE I KNOW YOU WOULDN'T DO IT, YOU'RE AN ONION. YOU THRIVE ON MOISTURE, THAT'S WHY YOU MOVED TO SEATTLE, REMEMBER? YOU DON'T KNOW WHAT IT'S LIKE TO BE A CUPCAKE. I CAN'T EVER GO TO HAWAII BECAUSE OF THE HUMIDITY. WHY, THEY EVEN HAVE TO PUT THEIR POSTAGE STAMPS IN THE FRIDGE. . . .NO, IT'S NOT COSMETIC. . .WELL, NO, MY INSURANCE WON'T PAY. . .YES, I KNOW IT'S EXPENSIVE. . . .WELL, I'M SORRY I CALLED YOU, TOO. I'VE ALWAYS SUPPORTED YOU, NO MATTER WHAT. . . IT SEEMS OUR RELATIONSHIP'S NOT WHAT I THOUGHT. . . .BYE.

HOW AWFUL.
REALLY? YES,
YES, I SEE. OH MY!
C.C., I CAN
SEE YOU NOW.

HI! I'M PATTY PRUNE, YOUR DEHYDRATION COUN-SELOR. SINCE YOU'RE FROM THE GRAIN FAMILY, TREATMENT WILL BE ON THE TOP TRAY WITH THE MINIMUM MOISTURE CONTACT. YOU'LL BE WITH US FOR EIGHT HOURS, SO WE'VE PROVIDED YOU WITH READING MATERIAL AND A TAPE DECK WITH EAR PHONES. YOUR INSURANCE WON'T PAY FOR YOUR REDUCTION. . . SINCE IT'S COSMETIC.
WELL, YES, BUT THAT PIECE OF CAKE SITTING OVER THERE? SHE SEEMS TO BE QUITE DISTRESSED.

WHAT DID SHE SAY TO YOU?
WELL, HER SISTER FELL APART FROM DEHY-DRATING TOO LONG, AND NOW SHE'S IN A HOSPITAL FOR LONG-TERM MULTIPLE FLAKING DISORDER.
SHE'S THE BOSS' DAUGHTER, SO THERE'S NOT MUCH I CAN DO EXCEPT TO TRY AND CONVINCE HER TO TAKE HER MEDICATIONS.

OH. I'M GLAD I DIDN'T GIVE HER MY PHONE NUMBER.
THAT'S A BIG TIME IMPROVEMENT ON MY PART.

NOW THERE ARE TEN FOLLOW-UP SESSIONS WHICH AREN'T INCLUDED IN THE ORIGINAL PRICE, SO WE WILL ADD........
WAIT A MINUTE. IF IT'S NOT INCLUDED, I DON'T WANT IT.
WELL, I DON'T KNOW IF WE CAN DO THAT. . . . . .YOU WON'T GET THE FULL EFFECT.
LOOK, I WANT THE FULL EFFECT AT THE ORIGINAL PRICE, OR I'M OUT OF HERE.
NO PROBLEM, SURE, OF COURSE.
WHOOPEE!!!

FOLLOWING DAY

If we didn't take every second
to be as old as we are,
it would always be too late,
or too soon,
to change.

Something to think about:
If we doubt that we can
rethink our lives - or are
afraid to try -
we will simply wind down
like the spring of a clock.

UH OH.
BOING!
WHOMP!

THIS IS FUN.
BOING!
BONK!
OOPS
BOING!
HELP
BONK!

CLUNK!
DARN IT
THAT'S BETTER

SSSSSSSSS
DO IT RIGHT AND SAFELY
AT OUR ATHLETIC & HEALTH FOOD CLUB
SPECIAL RATES FOR SPECIAL FOODS
TAKE CHARGE
OF YOUR LIFE
AND CALL NOW,
1-800-555-9274
DID YOU SEE
THE CELLULITE
ON THAT BURGER?

AEROBICS
"AND"
PLOP!
OTHER
HEALTHY STUFF
whoosh!

WELL,
HERE I
GO!
Athletic & Health
Club
SPECIAL RATES

ARE YOU HERE TO
LOSE WEIGHT, TOO?
WHY, DO YOU THINK
I NEED TO?
C.C. CUPCAKE?
I CAN SEE YOU
NOW.

IF YOU WANT TO REMAIN A HEALTHY AVOCADO, LOSE FIVE MORE POUNDS.
YES, AND NO MORE CELLULITE!
ISN'T THAT THE BURGER FROM YOUR AD?

DON'T FOLD ON ME NOW, FOLKS! KEEP GOING!
AND HERE WE HAVE OUR AEROBICS AREA. AS YOU CAN SEE, THE COOKIES USE IT FROM 10-11 A.M. CUPCAKES GET IT FROM 11 TO NOON, SO YOU CAN START TODAY.
Cookie
whamp!
UH HUH.

THIS IS THE TRACK YOU'LL BE RUNNING ON.
LOOKS LIKE FUN ....
....................I GUESS ....
SALT

In small steps there
are monumental gains.

No race has ever begun
at the finish line. It
began in the starting
blocks with the
imagination
you could
do it.

C.C.'S AEROBIC CLASS

I SHOULD DO AS MUCH AS POSSIBLE, CUZ' TODAY IS FREE. IF I CAN GO AROUND TWENTY MORE TIMES, I'LL ONLY HAVE TO COME HERE ONCE A WEEK.
OOPS, I'M OFF THE TRACK.
S
P
BAGEL
OH MY! C.C., DON'T PUSH IT. STOP FOR TODAY! OH MY.

C.C., I WANT YOU TO SIGN THIS. IF YOU HURT YOURSELF, WE ARE NOT RESPONSIBLE.

Don't try to do what
you're not capable
of doing.

Otherwise you might
wind up as a football
linebacker when you
only weigh 140 lbs.

Your mind may believe
in all possibility.
Your body won't
appreciate it.

IF YOU WANT TO BE
A HEALTHY CUPCAKE,
LOSE FIVE MORE OUNCES,
BUT, ...NOT NOW,
NOT TODAY.
OH, RATS!

I LOVE MYSELF.
I'M BEAUTIFUL.
I'M A GOOD CUPCAKE.
AND I'M NEVER GOING TO LET ANYONE SHAME ME OR GUILT ME INTO ANYTHING, EVER AGAIN. I AM THE MASTER OF MY LIFE. SO BE IT.

Don't kid yourself: Disappointment, like sandpaper, rubs away at all kinds of beliefs about people, places and things you thought would guarantee your well-being.

And often it hurts like hell.

Which only reveals how
much we layer over
what was a heavenly
piece of work in
the first place.

THE NEED TO WAKE UP

A WEEK LATER - AT WORK

SO, C.C.... WE'VE COMPLETELY ELIMINATED YOUR DEPARTMENT, SO WE NO LONGER HAVE A PLACE FOR YOU HERE. YOU'VE BEEN LAID OFF.
YOU'VE DONE A GREAT JOB THESE PAST FIFTEEN YEARS, SO WE WOULD LIKE TO PRESENT YOU WITH AN EXTRA WEEK'S SEVERANCE PAY.
UPPER MGT

UPPER MGT.

I FEEL SO USED.
click

TOO BAD SHE
COULDN'T LIVE
UP TO HER NAME.
TWINKI
GUM
LIVE SAVER
CLICK

PETER, I'M PERMANENTLY LAID OFF, AND I DON'T KNOW WHAT TO DO. I THINK I'M AHH, DEPRESSED - YEAH, THAT MUST BE IT.
SOUNDS LIKE YOU'VE NEVER ACKNOWLEDGED BEING DEPRESSED. INTERESTING.
HOW DEPRESSING.
I'LL BE RIGHT THERE. NO, IT'S NO PROBLEM. THINGS AREN'T GOING TOO WELL HERE, ANYWAY.

HOW DID YOU GET HERE?
SAME WAY I GET TO MY A.A. MEETINGS, A BORROWED BIKE. I HAVE SOMETHING TO SAY. AH, LET ME SEE IF I CAN RE-CALL THE EXACT WORDS . . .
AND HERE I THOUGHT SHE HAD IT ALL TOGETHER.

HMMM. OH YES, I REMEMBER. C.C., YOU SHOULDN'T FEEL SO BAD. AS MY A.A. GROUP SAYS, YOU'RE RIGHT WHERE YOU'RE SUPPOSED TO BE. AHHH, OH YES, AND THE UNIVERSE WORKS IN MYSTERIOUS WAYS, AND THAT SOMETIMES WE NEED A KICK IN THE BUTT TO GET US OUT OF OUR OLD RUTS SO WE CAN MOVE ONTO EVEN BIGGER AND BETTER THINGS.
THAT'S JUST ABOUT THE STUPIDEST THING I'VE EVER HEARD. READ MY LIPS . . .I'M OVER THIRTY AND I DON'T HAVE A JOB. A JOB, I MIGHT ADD, I'VE GIVEN MY LIFE TO FOR THE LAST FIFTEEN YEARS.

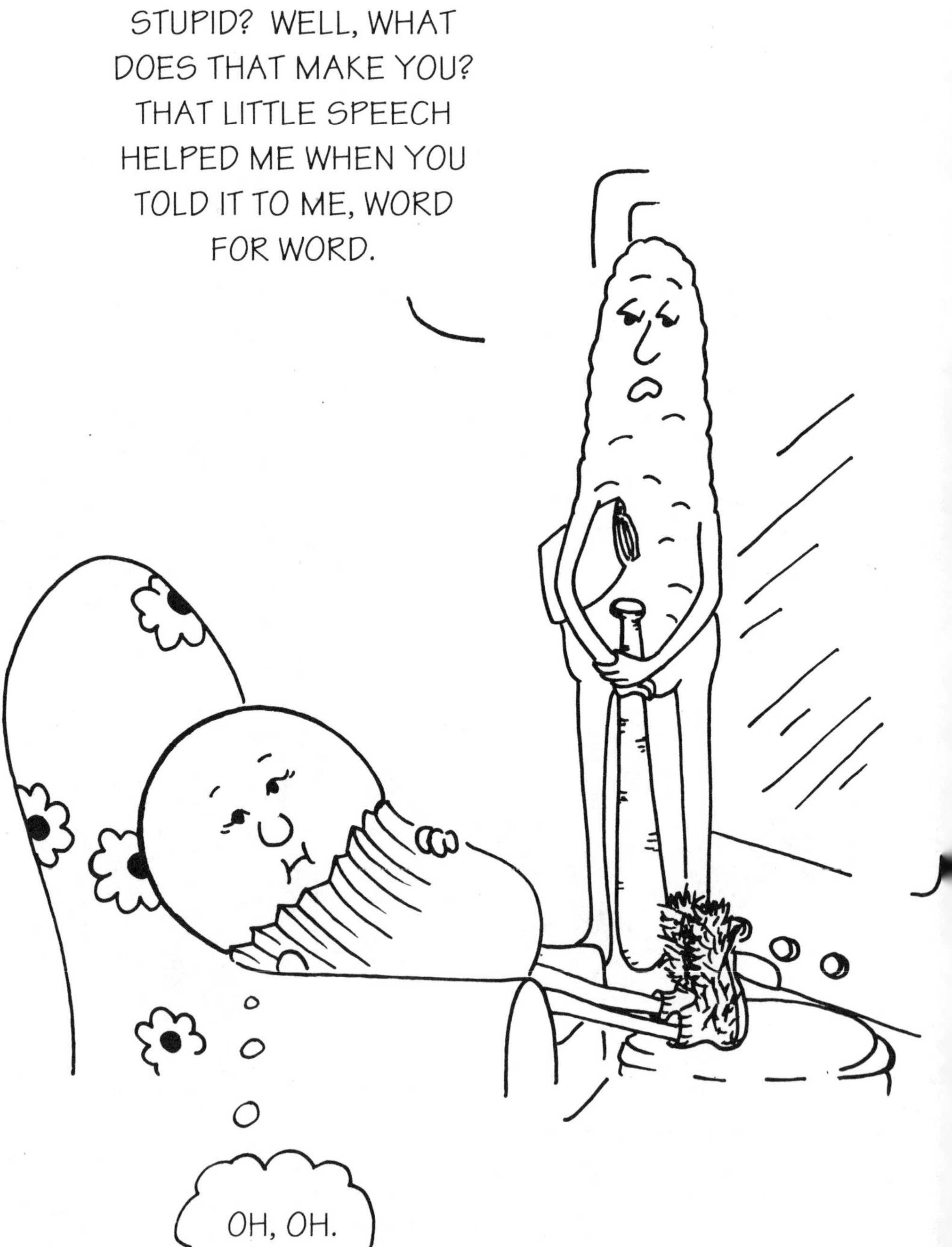
STUPID? WELL, WHAT DOES THAT MAKE YOU? THAT LITTLE SPEECH HELPED ME WHEN YOU TOLD IT TO ME, WORD FOR WORD.
OH, OH.

FIRST OF ALL, THIS IS THE BOOK YOU LOANED ME, "TO GET ON WITH YOUR LIFE - TRY DOING WHAT YOU LOVE." IT MIGHT HELP YOU AS MUCH AS IT'S HELPING ME.
WHAT'S WITH THE BAT? ARE YOU PLANNING TO BEAT ME OUT OF MY DEPRESSION?
THIS PLASTIC BAT IS A SAFE WAY TO EXPRESS YOUR ANGER BY BEATING IT ON A BED OR A CHAIR.

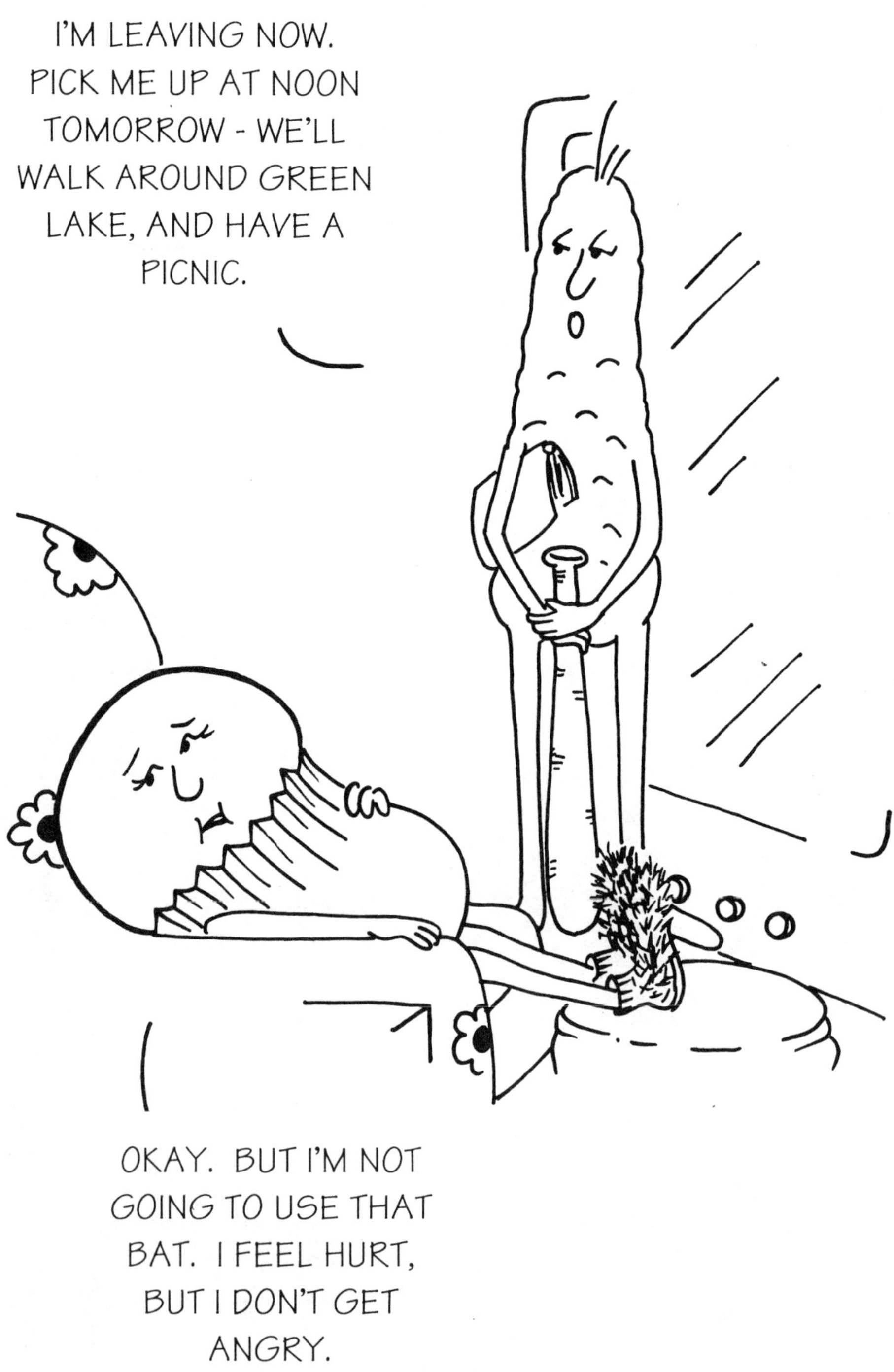
I'M LEAVING NOW. PICK ME UP AT NOON TOMORROW - WE'LL WALK AROUND GREEN LAKE, AND HAVE A PICNIC.
OKAY. BUT I'M NOT GOING TO USE THAT BAT. I FEEL HURT, BUT I DON'T GET ANGRY.

SHAME, GUILT, AND BITTERNESS FREQUENTLY COVER UP RESENTMENTS, WHICH IN TURN COVER ANGER.
WHEN ONE LOSES HIS OR HER HOME, JOB, ETC., IT'S NORMAL TO FEEL THAT LOSS. THAT INCLUDES ANGER.
WHOMP
WHOMP
WHOMP!

TIME TO MOVE ON

HOW DO YOU FEEL TODAY?
BETTER. I DID USE THE BAT. IT'S THE STRANGEST THING. AFTERWARDS, I FELT REALLY GOOD, ESPECIALLY MY BODY. DO YOU SUPPOSE EMOTIONAL PAIN CAN BE STORED IN OUR BODIES, AND . . .
C.C., DON'T COMPLICATE THIS.
Putt Putt
FLOWER BED QUIET

I GUESS I'VE HAD LOTS OF LOSSES, AND DIDN'T EVEN KNOW IT . . . . I WISH I HAD.
Putt
WE ALL HAVE REGRETS. YA KNOW, I DIDN'T BECOME A PICKLE BY CHOICE. ONCE I WAS A YOUNG, UPWARDLY MOBILE CUCUMBER, BUT MY CONSTANT USE OF ALCOHOL . . . . WELL, MY BODY HAD TO ADAPT. SOMETIMES WHEN OTHERS LOOK MY WAY, I FEEL THEY WONDER IF MY PICKLING WAS FROM A NORMAL PROCESS, OR OVERINDULGENCE.
WHERE'S THAT PUTT, PUTT, COMING FROM?

Putt Putt!
SSSSSSS
Yikes!
Putt
Zoom
Boing!

Putt!
Putt!
Putt!
STOP IT, YOU IDIOT! YOU'RE MAKING A MOUNTAIN OUT OF A MOLE HILL.

There is nothing so complex

as what we make it to be -

And there is nothing so

simple as to know this.

PETER, ISN'T THAT CUTE? A "WELL SEASONED COUPLE".
AND LOOK WHAT'S COMING RIGHT AT US - A "WELL-MATCHED COUPLE". NOW DON'T STARE.

YEAH, WOW - THAT'S SOME MATCH! I WONDER WHAT THAT MEANS, SEEING TWO UNUSUAL RELATIONSHIPS WITHIN SECONDS OF EACH OTHER.
YES, I AGREE, VERY UNUSUAL, VERY DIFFERENT..................YUP.
SOMETIMES THE THINGS THAT COME OUT OF HER MOUTH ARE BEYOND WEIRD.
OH, I GET IT. SHE'S HINTING ABOUT HAVING A RELATIONSHIP WITH ME. HOW CLEVER.
HEY, LET'S SIT BY THE WATER.
Pat Pat!
SOMEDAY I'D LIKE TO HAVE A RELATIONSHIP WITH SOMEONE, BUT I NEED TO HAVE A RELATIONSHIP WITH MYSELF FIRST.

LOVELY DAY, ISN'T IT?

YUP.
WHAT ARE YOU
FEEDING THE DOG?

WHY DO YOU ASK?

WELL. . . I THINK HE'S GETTING
. . . OH, . . . A LITTLE ON THE
PLUMP SIDE . . .KINDA, SORT OF.

SEEMS HEALTHY ENOUGH
TO ME. I FEED HIM
EVERYTHING I EAT.

WHAT!!!
THAT'S HIGH CHOLESTEROL.
JUST BECAUSE ANIMALS CAN
CROSS OVER DOESN'T MEAN
THEY CAN EAT LIKE WE DO.

WHOSE DOG IS THIS, ANYWAY?
JUST BECAUSE YOU BOUGHT
HIM DOESN'T GIVE YOU THE
RIGHT TO TELL ME HOW TO
CARE FOR HIM.

YEAH, WELL, I GUESS THAT MAKES
YOU RIGHT "ONE MORE TIME".

AND WHAT'S THAT
SUPPOSED TO MEAN?

OH, NOTHING. . . I JUST MEAN
YOU'RE USUALLY RIGHT.

REALLY?

YUP.

REALLY? REALLY? REALLY?

WELL, PETER, WHAT ARE WE GOING TO DO WITH THE REST OF OUR LIVES?

I DON'T KNOW. WHAT ARE WE GOING TO DO?

I ASKED YOU CUZ' I WANTED YOUR OPINION.

WELL, I STILL DON'T KNOW.

ME, NEITHER.

DITTO.

DITTO?

MEANS I AGREE.

WHY DO YOU ALWAYS AGREE WITH ME?

CUZ' I RESPECT YOUR OPINION?

WELL, GET SOME OF YOUR OWN. AND GIVE ME PERMISSION TO HAVE POOR JUDGEMENT.

ARE WE HAVING OUR FIRST FIGHT?

I HOPE SO.

MY NEW FRIEND, LOTTA LIMABEAN, IS GOING ON A WILDERNESS TREK, AND I DECIDED TO GO WITH.

ISN'T THAT JUST A BUNCH OF HALF-NAKED SISSY MALES BEATING DRUMS, STOMPING AROUND A FIRE? YA KNOW, MALE BONDING STUFF?

I DON'T KNOW ABOUT THAT. THIS WILDERNESS PROGRAM IS ABOUT CHALLENGING SITUATIONS, AND BUILDING TRUST AND CONFIDENCE. . . GETTING IN TOUCH WITH MY WARRIOR ENERGY.

OH. UH, OH, HERE IT COMES. WHY IT'S A PERSONAL OPINION! DO YOU WANT TO HEAR IT?

I THINK SO. . .

YOU'RE BEING TOTALLY IRRESPONSIBLE. YOU NEED TO GET ON UNEMPLOYMENT AND THEN LOOK FOR A JOB, NOT BE RUNNING AWAY.

I RESPECT YOUR OPINION, PETER, BUT THAT'S NOT WHAT I'M DOING. I'VE ALWAYS TRIED TO DO THE RIGHT THING FOR OTHERS. NOW IT'S MY TURN TO BE RESPONSIBLE TO MYSELF - NOT YOU, OR FRIENDS, OR FAMILY. FOR ME. JUST ME. SO FOR NOW, I'M GOING TO USE MY PENSION MONEY AND DO WHAT I NEED TO DO.

HMMM. I GUESS I WAS MOSTLY WORRYING THAT YOU'RE NOT GOING TO BE THERE FOR ME. WOW, THAT WAS PRETTY SELFISH!

OKAY.

DON'T COMPLICATE THIS.

Where is it said,
the path ends here,
and this is as far
as we can go.

Choose to find out
who you are.

When you're done,
you're being born.

What a wonderful
gift!

TO BE CONTINUED......................